The Man Who Sharpened Stones

A Fable of Continuous Improvement

Steve Aldridge

Published by Aldridge Performance Advisory LLC

Saint Charles, Missouri

First Edition

PAPERBACK ISBN: 979-8-9959845-1-1

EBOOK (PDF) ISBN: 979-8-9959845-0-4

Business / Leadership / Inspirational

Contents

For the man who is good at what he does and wonders, quietly, if good is enough.

For the woman who stands beside him and already knows the answer.

And for the five who walk alongside, the ones who help, the ones who hinder, and the ones who do both at once.

A Note Before the Story Begins

Most stories about success begin at the bottom. The hero has nothing, earns everything, and arrives at the top with his arms raised and the crowd cheering.

This is not that story.

This story begins in the middle, which is, if you think about it, where most of us actually live. Not at the bottom, not at the top, but somewhere in between, doing reasonably well, wondering what "better" might look like, and not entirely sure we deserve to find out.

Ray lived in the middle. He had built something real from honest work. He had a wife he loved, a business that ran, and a reputation that meant something in a town called Prescott.

And yet.

There was a feeling he could not name. A restlessness that lived in his chest like a stone he had swallowed years ago and never quite digested. Everything was fine. Everything was good, even.

But good, as Ray would come to learn, is sometimes the greatest obstacle to better.

This is the story of how he found that out.

— ✦ —

Part One: The Man in the Middle

The Town Called Prescott

Prescott was the kind of mid-sized American town that did not make the national news unless a storm blew through. It had a downtown with a few good restaurants and a coffee shop that had been there since before anyone could remember. It had a chamber of commerce that met every third Tuesday and a business community tight enough that everyone knew everyone, but large enough that you could still be surprised.

The business district on the east side of downtown was the heart of commercial life. Office buildings that were not quite towers. A row of storefronts along Main Street that cycled through tenants every few years, with a handful of anchors that had been there for decades. The smell of coffee and dry-cleaned suits and, in the summer, the faint green smell of the parks along the river.

Ray had grown up in Prescott. He was forty-three years old, broad-shouldered and steady, with the kind of face that people trusted on sight and the kind of handshake that meant something. He ran a performance advisory firm called Ray's Performance Advisory on the second floor of a building on Main Street. The firm handled business strategy, process improvement, and operational consulting for companies in the region. He had built it from a one-man practice out of a rented office into a firm with six employees, a steady book of clients, and a reputation for honest and grounded advice that had taken fifteen years to earn.

He had done all of this without cutting corners or overselling. He had worked hard and long and steadily, and the firm reflected it.

By any reasonable measure, Ray was a success.

And yet, on the morning this story begins, he sat at his desk before his first client call and stared at his open laptop without reading it, felt the stone in his chest, and could not have told you why.

Estella

His wife's name was Estella, and she was the kind of person who noticed things without making a production of noticing them.

She noticed, for instance, that Ray had been staring at the same email for twenty minutes without responding. She noticed the particular set of his shoulders that meant he was thinking about something he had not yet decided to say out loud. She noticed the way he had eaten breakfast that morning, present in body, somewhere else in mind.

She set a fresh cup of coffee on his desk, sat down across from him in the chair their youngest had claimed as the reading chair years ago, and said nothing.

This was one of the many things Ray loved about Estella. She did not poke at silence. She simply sat in it with you, which made it easier to eventually break.

"I don't know what I'm doing wrong," he said, after a while.

"Nothing," she said, without looking up from her phone, where she was reviewing her morning calendar.

"Then why does it feel like something?"

She set the phone down and looked at him. Her eyes were calm and direct, the eyes of someone who had long ago made peace with the difference between what she could control and what she could not. "Because nothing wrong and nothing missing are two different things," she said.

He looked at her.

"You haven't done anything wrong, Ray. The firm is good. Our life is good. But you are the kind of man who is always asking whether good is as good as it could be." She picked up her coffee. "That is not a flaw. It is who you are. The question is what you do with it."

"What should I do with it?"

She smiled, small and certain, in the way she smiled when she already knew the answer and was waiting for him to find it himself. "Go for a walk," she said. "You always think better when you walk. Leave the phone."

He did. He walked out into downtown that morning with no particular destination, and that is when things began to change.

The Stone at the Well

There was a woman who sat every morning on the bench outside the old coffee shop across from the courthouse square. Her name was Nona, and she had been sitting there for so long that most of the regulars no longer saw her. She had become part of the scenery, like the iron bench itself or the oak tree whose roots had begun to lift the sidewalk beside it.

Nona was somewhere past seventy, though she had the alertness of someone half that age. She had run a small business consulting practice in Prescott for forty years before retiring, and before that she had worked in half a dozen industries across half a dozen cities. She came to the bench each morning with a large coffee and the kind of patient calm that only comes from having genuinely stopped caring what people think.

Ray had walked past her a hundred times. He stopped this morning, for the first time.

He was not sure why. Something in her expression, alert and still at once, the way a hawk is still, made him slow down.

"You look like a man carrying something heavy," she said, before he could speak.

"I don't have anything to carry," he said.

"No," she agreed. "That's the problem, isn't it."

He stared at her. Then he sat down on the far end of the bench, which he had not planned to do, and found himself talking.

He told her about the firm, what he had built, how it ran, what it produced. He told her about the email he had not been reading. He told her about the stone in his chest that had no name.

She listened without interrupting. She sipped her coffee. She looked at him over the rim of the cup with eyes that were older than her face.

When he finished, she said: "You have built a good thing. And somewhere inside you, you know it could be a better thing. And you are afraid, not of failure, you have survived failure before, you are afraid of the work it would take to find out where better is."

Ray was quiet for a moment. "That seems harsh."

"Does it feel inaccurate?"

He thought about it. "No."

"Good. The truth usually stings a little at first. It is only the lies that feel comfortable right away." She set down her cup. "Tell me, when something goes wrong in your firm, what do you do?"

"I fix it," he said.

"And then?"

"And then I move on."

Nona nodded slowly, as if this confirmed something. "And do the same things go wrong again? A different form, perhaps, but the same root cause?"

Ray opened his mouth to say no. Then he closed it.

He thought about the client onboarding problems that resurfaced every six months. He thought about the billing disputes that arrived in patterns he had never stopped to analyze. He thought about the recurring tension with one of his senior consultants, the same conflict cycling back every quarter with different surface details but the same essential shape underneath.

"Yes," he said. "Some things do."

"Because you fix the symptom and move on," Nona said. "You do not ask why it happened. You do not study the break. You replace what broke and return to work." She folded her hands in her lap. "That is very common. It is not a character failing. It is a habit. And habits can be changed."

"What should I do instead?"

"Ask why," she said. "Before you move on. Every time something breaks, a process, a client relationship, a plan, sit with the wreckage for a moment before you clean it up. Ask what caused it. Then ask why that caused it. Keep asking why until you reach the real root of the problem, not just the surface of it. Write it all down." She paused. "And then, Ray, look around you. This city is full of teachers. You have been walking past them for years."

She stood and tucked her coffee cup under her arm.

"Come back when you have something to tell me," she said. And she walked back inside the coffee shop.

Ray sat on the bench for a long time after she left.

On his way back to the office, he passed five people he had known for years, and looked at each of them, for the first time, as if they might have something to teach him.

Part Two: The Five

Paul, Who Moved Fast and Broke Things

The first of the five was Paul, and he was the kind of friend who made life more interesting and more complicated in equal measure.

Paul ran a regional marketing and media company out of a glass-fronted office two blocks from Ray's. He was everywhere at once, on social media, at every chamber event, at a conference in Denver, and a networking dinner, all in the same week. He had launched four businesses by the time he was forty-five. Two had done well. One had done spectacularly, briefly. One had ended in a lawsuit he did not like to discuss. He wore all of this history like a badge of experience rather than a scar of failure.

Ray had known Paul since their thirties. They had met at a chamber breakfast and discovered they shared a parking space, a taste for good bourbon, and a complete inability to leave a business problem alone once they had spotted it. The friendship had been easy and energizing ever since.

When Ray told Paul about his restlessness over lunch at their usual spot, Paul leaned forward immediately.

"You need to scale," he said. "New service lines. New markets. You are thinking too local, there are companies two states over that need exactly what you do and do not have anyone doing it."

"I am not sure scaling is the..."

"Look at what Landen did with his accounting firm. Opened three satellite offices in eighteen months. The guy is printing money."

"Landen also went through two partners and had a tax audit," Ray said.

Paul waved his hand. "That is the cost of moving fast. You cannot build something bigger without some friction."

And this was the thing about Paul: he was not wrong, exactly. Growth was not a bad idea. Ambition was not inherently foolish. The problem was that Paul had never met a risk he did not like, and his enthusiasm for moving forward had a way of papering over the need for careful preparation and honest assessment.

Ray left the lunch energized but vaguely uneasy.

That evening, he told Estella about it.

She listened carefully. Then she said, "Paul loves you. And Paul's advice is always built for Paul. His way of improving is to go faster. That works for him, sometimes. Is that what works for you?"

Ray thought about it. "No," he said. "I don't think it is."

"Then take what's useful, that change is possible, and growth is not inherently wrong, and leave the rest."

He nodded. Estella had a gift for this: separating the good part of something from the part that was just noise.

Nick, Who Polished the Surface

The second of the five was Nick, who was in many ways the opposite of Paul.

Nick owned a high-end commercial real estate brokerage in downtown Prescott, polished, precise, and deeply attentive to how things appeared. His office looked like it belonged in an architecture magazine. His suits were impeccable. His client gifts arrived in boxes tied with actual ribbon. Everything about Nick's professional life was designed to project a specific image, and to his credit, it worked; he was one of the most successful brokers in the region.

He was also, Ray sometimes thought, more interested in the brand of success than in the practice of it.

When Ray shared his restlessness with Nick over coffee, Nick nodded thoughtfully and said, "What you need is a refresh. Updated website, sharper LinkedIn presence, maybe a rebrand of the firm. Ray's Performance Advisory is solid, but it does not pop. First impressions drive decisions, clients are searching for you online before they ever pick up the phone."

It was not terrible advice. Ray's website was, in fact, three years out of date.

But when he gently pressed further, asking about the deeper problems, the recurring process failures, the cycles of tension with his senior consultant, Nick grew vague.

"Those are internal details," he said, with the mild dismissiveness of someone who considered operations a lesser concern. "The big picture is what matters. If your market presence is strong, the operational stuff sorts itself out."

Ray left with a list of cosmetic improvements and a feeling that something important had been left unaddressed.

He did update the website. It looked better. It did not move the stone in his chest.

What Nick had taught him, without meaning to, was the difference between improving the image of a thing and improving the thing itself. Both mattered. But they were not the same, and the first could easily become a way of avoiding the second.

Cole, Who Had Been There Before

The third of the five was Cole, and he was unlike anyone else in Ray's life.

Cole was a local attorney in his early sixties who had built a practice focused on families, small businesses, and people who needed someone in their corner and could not afford to hire a large downtown firm that billed by the tenth of an hour. He had started from scratch after leaving a regional law firm in his late thirties, a decision that had cost him a significant salary and, briefly, his confidence, and had spent the past two decades building something smaller, quieter, and by his own measure far more meaningful.

He was one of the most respected people in Prescott, not because he was famous but because he was known. People trusted him the way they trusted a good family doctor, not for the credentials on the wall, but because he had been there when things were hard and had never flinched.

He was not easy to talk to, exactly. He had a habit of waiting until you finished speaking and then staying quiet for longer than felt comfortable before he responded. Many people found this unsettling. Ray had always found it clarifying.

When Ray came to him, they met occasionally for lunch, a habit that had grown out of a shared client referral years earlier. Cole listened to all of it without expression. The restlessness. Nona's challenge. Paul's enthusiasm. Nick's surface advice.

Then he was silent for a long moment.

"What are you actually afraid of?" he said finally.

"I told you. I feel like the firm could be better, but I don't..."

"That's what you said. I asked what you're afraid of."

Ray stopped.

The question sat between them like something solid.

"That if I look closely enough," he said slowly, "I'll find that I've been doing it wrong for years. That the problems are not just in the process; they are in me. The way I lead. The decisions I've made. The habits I've never questioned." He paused. "That is harder to fix than a website or a new service line."

Cole nodded once. "Yes," he said. "And that is exactly why most people never look." He leaned forward slightly. "I left my old firm because I had known for almost two years it was not right, not for me, and not for the clients we were supposed to be serving. I knew it. I kept finding reasons not to look at it honestly. By the time I finally did, I had wasted two years and burned more goodwill than I had to spare."

He let that sit.

"When I started my own practice, the first thing I changed was not my specialty or my fee structure. It was my willingness to be wrong. I started asking myself every single week: what did I get wrong this week? Not to beat myself up. Just to see clearly." He sat back. "That one change made every other change possible. Because you cannot fix what you are protecting from scrutiny and unwilling to expose."

Ray wrote that down when he got back to the office.

You cannot fix what you are protecting from scrutiny.

Estella read it over his shoulder that evening and said nothing. But she put her hand briefly on his shoulder as she passed, which meant more than words would have.

Moose, Who Pulled Toward Darkness

The fourth of the five was Moose, and he is the hardest one to write about honestly.

Moose was one of Ray's oldest friends. They had worked together in their late twenties at another firm, shared lean years and good ones, and the bond between them was real and deep. But somewhere along the way, Moose had developed a bitterness toward the professional world that had slowly turned into something more dangerous.

Moose was not a bad person. That is important to say. He ran a small insurance agency in Prescott, worked hard, and treated his clients fairly. He genuinely believed what he told Ray, and he told it from a place of real concern. But Moose had been let down by the business world too many times: a partner who had defrauded him, a market shift that had gutted his commissions, a loan that had taken five years to climb out of, and he had concluded from all of it that the game was largely rigged. That the people who succeeded had either unusual luck or questionable ethics. That the wisest response was a guarded, defensive contentment with what you already had.

When Ray shared his desire for improvement, Moose's response was measured, kind, and quietly harmful.

"You've built something real, Ray. Don't let anyone talk you into believing it's not enough." He gestured in the general direction of the business district. "All this improvement and growth and optimization culture, half of it is consultants and coaches selling solutions to problems they invented. The guys I've watched chase the next level usually end up worse off than when they started. You know what you have. Protect it."

There was just enough truth in this to make it dangerous.

Ray did know what he had. It was worth protecting. Chasing change for its own sake was foolish. And some of the self-improvement industry was exactly as hollow as Moose described.

But as Ray drove home that evening, he noticed something uncomfortable. Moose's words had felt soothing. They had given him permission to stop. And the fact that they felt so good was, itself, a warning sign.

He thought about what Cole had said, about protecting things from scrutiny. Moose was offering him a very comfortable protection. The question was whether he would take it.

He talked to Estella that night for a long time.

"Moose loves you," she said. "And Moose has been genuinely hurt. When someone has been hurt enough times, they start building walls and calling them wisdom." She was quiet for a moment. "His walls are his. You don't have to live inside them."

Ray lay awake for a while after that, in the dark, and made a quiet decision. He would not let Moose's fear become his own. He would keep what was real in what Moose said, caution was not foolishness, contentment had value, and not all growth was good, and he would leave the resignation behind.

It was a hard decision to make about a friend he loved. But it was the right one.

Mitch, Who Saw What Others Missed

The fifth of the five was Mitch, and he was the sharpest observer Ray had ever known.

Mitch was a corporate attorney who had practiced in Prescott for over twenty years, building a reputation that extended well beyond the region. His firm handled mergers, regulatory matters, and complex business transactions for some of the largest companies in the state. He was the kind of lawyer that companies called when the situation was serious, not the everyday kind of serious, but the kind where the wrong decision could end careers or unravel what had taken decades to build.

What made Mitch unusual was not his legal skill, though that was considerable. It was his habit of watching organizations from the inside out. Every case gave him a new vantage point, a different company, a different leadership team, a different set of strengths and hidden cracks. After two decades of this, he had developed an almost uncanny ability to read the shape of a business from the outside, the way a doctor can sense a patient's health in the way they carry themselves before a single word is spoken.

Ray had known Mitch through the chamber and shared civic work for years, but they had never spoken deeply until the afternoon they ended up at tables next to each other at a downtown lunch spot and Mitch said, without any introduction:

"You have been distracted lately. What is going on with the firm?"

Ray blinked. They had exchanged maybe three hundred words total over the years. He opened his mouth to offer the standard fine, just busy, and instead found himself telling the truth.

Mitch listened the way he probably listened in depositions, completely still, completely present, giving nothing away.

When Ray finished, Mitch said, "Your firm has a structural problem that is also a leadership problem. Those are usually the same problem."

"What do you mean?"

"You have built a practice around your own judgment. Your clients trust Ray, not Ray's Performance Advisory. That is an asset and a liability. The asset is that your reputation is strong. The liability is that nothing in the firm works as well without you, which means you cannot scale, cannot take a real vacation, and cannot delegate anything that matters without anxiety." He picked up his coffee. "I see this constantly in the companies I work with. The founder becomes the bottleneck. The business grows to the size of one person's bandwidth and then stops."

Ray absorbed this. "What would you do?"

"I would start by watching the firm the way an outside observer would. Look at your own processes honestly. Where are you the only person who can do something? Where do decisions wait for you that should not? Where are you solving the same problems over and over because the system that should prevent them does not exist yet?" He paused. "The goal is not to remove yourself from the work. It is to build a firm that runs on principles and process, one where trust and accountability are built into how the team operates, not just into your presence."

"How do you see all this from the outside?" Ray asked.

"I have watched a lot of companies make every mistake available," Mitch said simply. "After enough repetitions, the patterns become obvious. The hard part is not seeing them from the outside. The hard part is seeing them from the inside, which is where you are." He set down his cup. "Your assumptions about how the firm works have become invisible to you. That is your biggest challenge right now."

Ray drove back to the office with Mitch's words running through his mind, and by the time he parked he had pulled out the small notebook he had started carrying and written two questions at the top of a fresh page:

What does Ray's Performance Advisory need that I have not given it?

What am I doing every day that only I should be doing, and what am I doing that I should have handed off years ago?

Estella saw the notebook that evening and raised an eyebrow.

"New habit," he said.

"Keep it," she said. "It suits you."

Part Three: The Work

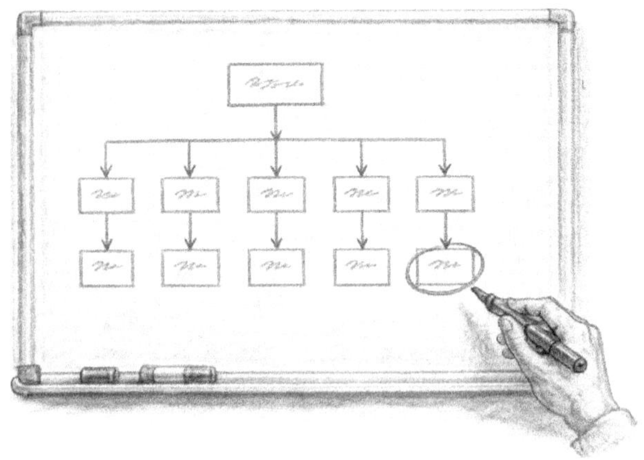

Ray Watches Himself Work

Inspired by Mitch's challenge and armed with his notebook, Ray spent the following week doing something he had never done before: watching himself work.

Not in a self-conscious way, not as a performance, but as an observation. He tried to see his own habits the way an outside consultant might. He tracked how he spent his time, noted when he made decisions by reflex rather than by thought, and paid attention to where the day flowed smoothly and where it broke down and why.

What he found was more than he expected.

He found that he spent nearly two hours a day on administrative and coordination tasks that his office manager, Tom, was entirely capable of handling; Ray held onto them not because he was better at them, but because he had always done them and had never thought to question it. Two hours a day was ten hours a week. More than a full working day, every single week, spent on work that did not require him.

He found that the firm's client onboarding process was different every time, not because each situation was different, but because no one had ever written down a standard process. Every onboarding ran on informal memory and whoever happened to be available. He had assumed this was fine because clients had not complained. But when he looked more carefully, he found three clients in the past year who had gone quiet within the first sixty days. He had chalked this up to a bad fit. He now suspected it was friction.

He found that the recurring tension with Tom, a capable, ambitious young man who had been with the firm for three years, followed a very specific pattern. It always surfaced when Ray gave direction without context. Tom was not someone who followed instructions well in a vacuum. He was someone who worked brilliantly when he understood the reasoning behind what he was being asked to do. Ray had never noticed this because he had never thought of Tom as someone who needed a different kind of leadership. He had simply led him the same way he led everyone, efficiently and clearly, but without explanation.

He brought each of these observations back to the group, one by one, over a series of evenings at a corner table of a downtown restaurant where the five had begun meeting informally. They were drawn together partly by curiosity and partly by the force of Ray's earnest engagement with his own improvement.

Even Paul sat still for these conversations. Even Moose came, though he often sat with his arms crossed and said little.

It was in these meetings that something began to form, not just Ray's improvement, but something larger. A shared practice. A common language. The group began to turn the same honest eye on their own work, each in their own way, and the insights multiplied.

The Lesson of the Record

It was a retired CPA named Maureen who introduced Ray to the discipline of the written record.

Ray had been referred to Maureen by a mutual client. She had retired from practice but still consulted informally, and her reputation for meticulous recordkeeping was legendary among the accountants and bookkeepers in Prescott. They met over coffee and Ray found Maureen exactly as advertised: precise, unhurried, and deeply interested in patterns.

"What do you track?" Ray asked, after Maureen had listened to the state of Ray's Performance

Advisory with the focused patience of a woman who had heard a great many business problems.

"Everything," Maureen said simply. "Revenue by client, by service line, by month. Time spent versus time billed. Client acquisition source. Retention rates by year. Referral patterns. Complaints. Compliments." She paused. "Every single day, for thirty-one years."

Ray was quiet for a moment. "What does thirty-one years of data tell you?"

"It tells me patterns that are invisible without it," Maureen said. "Human memory is not a reliable instrument. It remembers what felt important and forgets what seemed small. But the small things are often where the real information lives." She looked at Ray steadily. "I would bet you do not know your client retention rate by year."

"I know it's good."

"Good is not a number." Maureen said it without unkindness. "Good is a feeling. Feelings change with your mood. Numbers do not."

Ray bought a new notebook on the way back to the office and started that afternoon.

He also, at Maureen's suggestion, built a simple tracking spreadsheet, nothing elaborate, just consistent. Client activity, billing trends, time allocation, team capacity. Within six weeks, the data had shown him three things he had not known: his best referral source was not who he thought it was, his most profitable service line was not his most time-consuming one, and client turnover was concentrated almost entirely in a single industry he had been trying to grow.

Estella watched him working on the spreadsheet one evening at the kitchen table and poured him a cup of coffee without being asked.

"You seem lighter," she said.

"I feel like I can see things I couldn't see before," he said.

"That is what happens," she said, "when you stop carrying everything in your head."

Five Whys

Not long after his conversation with Maureen, Ray sat down with Tom to work through the onboarding problem. Three clients had gone quiet in the first sixty days. That was not a coincidence. That was a pattern. And patterns, Ray had come to believe, always had a root cause worth finding.

"Let's not just fix it," Ray said. "Let's understand it."

He had learned a simple technique from a process improvement book Nona had pressed into his hand the week before, a method called the Five Whys. It had been developed decades earlier within Toyota's manufacturing system and had been used widely in Lean practice ever since. The idea was straightforward: when a problem surfaces, do not stop at the obvious answer. Ask why it happened. Then ask why that happened.

Keep asking why, up to five times if needed, until you reach the actual source of the problem rather than just the nearest symptom.

Ray and Tom worked through it together at the whiteboard.

The clients had gone quiet. Why? Because they had not heard from the firm in the first thirty days. Why? Because no one had a documented follow-up process. Why? Because onboarding was handled differently by each consultant. Why? Because there was no shared standard, each person had developed their own informal approach over time. Why? Because Ray had never created one. He had assumed that experienced consultants would naturally stay in sync.

They sat with that last answer for a moment.

"So the problem," Tom said carefully, "is not that we are careless. It is that we never built the system in the first place."

"Right," Ray said. "And because we never built it, we have been solving the same problem in different ways, over and over, and calling it done each time."

That conversation was the beginning of something important. It was not just a solution to an onboarding gap. It was a model, a collaborative way of approaching problems that Ray began to carry into every part of the firm. Instead of handing Tom an answer, he started handing him a question. Instead of diagnosing problems alone in his office, he brought the team into the process.

The culture of the firm began to shift, slowly but unmistakably, from one where Ray solved things to one where the team solved things together.

Trust deepened. Accountability spread. People began to own not just their tasks but their outcomes.

The Trouble with Paul

Three months into Ray's practice of improvement, Paul came to him with a proposal.

A regional consulting firm in a neighboring city was looking to sell. It was smaller than Ray's Performance Advisory but had a different client base and two strong consultants. A strategic acquisition, Paul said. It would double their footprint overnight, open new markets, and position Ray's Performance Advisory as a regional player instead of a local one. He had already spoken to the owner informally. The price was reasonable. The timing was right.

It was exciting. Ray felt the pull of it, the scope, the ambition, the possibility of something genuinely larger.

He also felt, underneath the excitement, the familiar pattern of how things went with Paul: fast decision, bold move, figure out the details once you are already moving.

He did not say yes or no immediately. He went back to his office and wrote in his journal:

Paul's proposal. Acquisition. What do I actually know about this? What do I not know? What would I need to know before this was a sound decision rather than just an exciting one?

He made a list. It was long. He worked through each item over the following two weeks: the acquisition financials, the cultural fit, the integration costs, the capacity of his current team to absorb the change, and the risks if the two consultants decided to leave.

What he found was not disqualifying. But it was sobering. The asking price was fair on paper but assumed a client retention rate that historical data from similar deals did not support. One of the two consultants was, by informal accounts in the industry, already looking for other opportunities. The integration would require Tom to take on responsibilities he was not yet ready for.

He brought all of this to Paul, carefully, respectfully, with the analysis laid out clearly.

Paul studied it for a long moment.

"You would have said yes three months ago," he said. Not accusingly. Just observationally.

"Yes," Ray agreed. "I would have said yes because it felt exciting, because I trust you, and because I had not done the work of understanding what I was actually agreeing to."

Paul was quiet.

"The idea is not bad," Ray said. "But the timing is wrong and there are conditions that need to be met first. If we address the retention risk, confirm the consultant situation, and wait until Tom is ready for the operational load, I would like to revisit it in six months."

Paul looked at him for a long moment. Then, slowly, he smiled, a different kind of smile than his usual quick grin. Slower. More considered. "Nobody has ever pushed back on me with an actual analysis before," he said.

"Did it help?"

"It's annoying," Paul said. "But yes. It helped."

The acquisition was tabled. Six months later, when they revisited it, the asking price had changed, one of the consultants had in fact left, and Ray's instinct about the timing proved sound. They passed on it altogether and instead hired one strong independent consultant who had come from the target firm, the talent without the overhead.

It was the beginning of Paul becoming something more than just an exciting friend. It was the beginning of Paul becoming a genuinely useful one.

What Moose Was Really Saying

The conversation with Moose was harder.

It came on a Friday evening in late October when the two of them were at the bar of a restaurant they had been going to for fifteen years, with cold beers and the comfortable quiet of old friendship.

Moose had been watching Ray's changes from a distance, with what Ray read as a mix of pride and something more complicated underneath.

"You're different," Moose said finally.

"I've been working on some things."

"I know." A pause. "Are you happy?"

It was such a simple question that it stopped Ray cold.

"I think so," he said. "More than I was."

Moose turned his glass in his hands. "I wasn't trying to hold you back," he said. "When I said what I said. About protecting what you have."

"I know."

"I've just watched good men lose everything chasing more. Men who had enough and did not know it. Men who let someone convince them that what they had built was not sufficient." His voice was even, but there was an old grief in it that Ray recognized.

Ray thought about the partnership Moose had been part of in his late thirties, the one that had collapsed badly and taken a significant part of Moose's savings with it. Both of them had been close to that situation. Ray had watched it happen from the outside.

"I remember," Ray said quietly.

"So that is what I was talking about. Not that you should not grow. Just know what you are protecting while you do it."

"That is good advice," Ray said. "That is actually very good advice. The problem was not what you said. It was what I almost did with it."

Moose looked at him.

"I almost used it as permission to stop looking," Ray said. "And stopping looking is not the same as protecting what matters."

"What is the difference?"

"Protecting what matters means knowing what matters. Being intentional about it. Growing in ways that strengthen it." Ray paused, finding the words as he spoke them. "To stop looking means being afraid to see things as they are. Calling that caution instead of fear."

Moose absorbed this in silence.

"What happened with the partnership was not because you tried to grow," Ray said gently. "It happened because the wrong questions went unasked for too long. Because nobody wanted to look at what was actually there."

The old grief moved across Moose's face. Then, slowly, something that looked like relief.

"I've been protecting myself from the wrong thing," Moose said.

"Maybe," Ray said. "I've done the same. Just in different ways."

They sat in the comfortable silence of old friends who have just told each other something true.

It was the beginning of Moose, slowly and on his own terms, letting a few of his walls come down.

Part Four: The Question That Changed Everything

The Night of the Journal

It was a Tuesday in December when Ray sat down to write in his journal and found himself writing something he had not planned to write.

He had intended to review the week, client updates, a pending proposal, a staffing question he had been putting off. Instead, his pen moved to the top of a fresh page and wrote:

What is success?

He stared at the question.

He had been improving the firm. He had been a better leader to Tom. He had been more deliberate with Paul. He had been more honest with himself, in the daily practice of the journal, more honest than he had perhaps ever been. The stone in his chest had grown lighter.

But the question that now looked back at him from the page was larger than any of those things.

What is success?

Not what it was for Paul, or Cole, or Moose, or anyone else. For him. For Ray, specifically, in this life, in this town, with this work and this history and this wife and this one particular, unrepeatable existence.

He wrote for a long time that night.

He wrote about money, which mattered, but not as the main point. That financial security was a foundation, not a destination. That he wanted enough to live without fear, enough to provide for Estella and the kids, and enough to be generous when generosity was called for. Not more than that. More than that, in his honest assessment, would not make him meaningfully happier.

He wrote about work, that he needed it to be meaningful, not just profitable. That the days when he felt most alive were not the days with the highest billings but the days when he had helped a client solve a problem that genuinely mattered to them. When a business owner had come to him in real trouble and left with a clear path forward. When Tom had grown noticeably more confident under better leadership and had taken on a challenge that six months earlier he would have avoided altogether.

He wrote about his marriage, that Estella was not separate from his success but central to it. That a life built without her full flourishing in it would be hollow regardless of what else it contained. That he had been, in the years when the firm consumed everything, less present than she deserved and less aware of that than he should have been.

He wrote about purpose, and here his pen slowed, because the word was large and the feeling was real, but the shape of it was hard to put into words. He believed, in a quiet and undemonstrative way, that his life was not entirely his own. That he had been given certain strengths, a capacity for steadiness, for honest dealing, for the kind of long-term trust that came from never cutting corners, and that these were not accidental. That they came with an obligation to use them well. Not to be extraordinary. Just to be faithful with what he had been given.

He did not know if this was faith in any formal sense. He knew it was not nothing.

He wrote: I think I am here for something. Not something grand. Something specific. Something that only my particular life, lived well, can accomplish. I do not know yet exactly what it is. But I think the practice of improvement, the daily honest asking of whether I am doing what I am here to do, is the closest thing I have to finding out.

He closed the journal.

Estella was already asleep. He sat in the quiet for a while, listening to the house settle around him, feeling the stone in his chest, not gone exactly, but changed. From a burden into something more like an anchor. Something that held him to the ground of what mattered.

He slept better that night than he had in years.

The Conversation at the Bench

He went back to Nona.

It was January, cold enough that she had moved from her outdoor bench to a corner table just inside the coffee shop window, where she could still see the street. She looked, if possible, even more alert than usual in the pale winter light.

"You have been working," she said, as he sat down.

"For months," he said. He ordered a coffee. "I have something to tell you."

"Tell me."

He told her about the journal. About the five, what each of them had taught him and what each of them had tried, rightly or wrongly, to give him. About Tom and the acquisition and the tracking spreadsheet. About the Five Whys sessions with the team and the night in December.

Nona listened without interrupting. When he finished, she was quiet for a moment.

"You wrote: I am here for something," she said. "What do you think it is?"

"I do not know exactly. But I think it has something to do with the people around me getting better. Not just the firm. Tom is genuinely better, not just more productive, but more confident. Moose is a little less afraid. Paul is making more careful decisions. Estella," He paused. "Estella says I listen better. That I am more present." He looked at his hands around the coffee cup. "I have not done anything dramatic. I have not transformed into a different person. But the people closest to me are doing better. And I think that might be the shape of what I am here for."

"That is not a small thing," Nona said.

"It feels small compared to what Paul wants."

"Paul wants what Paul wants. You are not Paul." She looked at him steadily. "In all the reading and journaling and conversations, what has actually made the most difference? Not the most interesting thing. The thing that changed your life."

Ray thought about it for a long moment.

"Asking why," he said. "And being willing to hear the answer even when it points back at me."

"And what is the hardest part of that?"

"Doing it every day. When I am tired. When it would be easier to move on. When the answer is uncomfortable." He paused. "It is easy to be curious when something goes dramatically wrong. It is much harder when everything is just fine."

"Yes," she said. "That is the whole of it. The practice is not the dramatic moments. It is the ordinary days, the days when nothing breaks, when the numbers look reasonable, when the temptation is to close the laptop and say good enough." She sipped her coffee. "The person who asks why on those days, when nothing forces them to, that person improves at a rate that no one driven only by crisis can match."

Ray pulled on his coat to leave.

"Thank you," he said. "For that first conversation."

"You stopped yourself," she said. "I just gave you a place to sit."

Part Five: The Practice Spreads

The Gathering

Word travels in a business community the way it always has, through referrals, coffee meetings, and the quiet accumulation of observed results.

Word had gotten around about Ray.

Not dramatic word. Not the kind of story that ends up in a business journal. Just the quiet, persistent word of people who noticed: something had changed at Ray's Performance Advisory. The work was sharper. The client communication was more consistent. The young consultant there, Tom, had grown into someone you called with a complex problem because he was genuinely good at working through it.

People started asking Ray questions.

First it was a woman named Robin who ran a small manufacturing business and had been watching her margins compress for two years without being able to explain why. Then a young financial planner named Amy who was working hard, billing well, and somehow always behind. Then an old client named Silvia who ran a catering business and had never quite forgiven Ray for a scheduling mix-up three years earlier that she brought up whenever the opportunity presented itself.

Ray began meeting with them informally, first one-on-one, then as a loose group, in a private dining room at a downtown restaurant that the owner offered in exchange for Ray helping her think through her business finances. Once a week, on Thursday evenings, eight or ten people gathered around a long table with their problems and their questions.

The five came too: Paul, Nick, Cole, Moose, and Mitch, each one occupying their characteristic position in the room.

Paul arrived early, talked energetically, and with each passing week listened more and instructed less.

Nick came impeccably dressed and gradually stopped hiding behind the language of brand and presentation.

Cole sat near the end of the table and waited for the right moment, then said the thing no one else was willing to say, usually about risk, usually about what a client relationship was actually worth, and often about what the law could and could not protect.

Moose came reluctantly at first and sat near the back with his arms crossed. Then, slowly, he began to contribute, a cautionary pattern recognized, a risk flagged, the hard-won wisdom of someone who had paid close attention to how things fall apart.

Mitch sat in the middle and watched everything with the quiet attention of someone who had spent twenty years reading rooms. When he spoke, people listened, not because he was loud, but because he was almost always right.

Ray ran the meetings by asking questions rather than providing answers. He had learned, from all of them, that the quality of the question shaped the quality of the outcome.

What happened? Why did it happen? What would you do differently? What are you not looking at?

The last question was always the hardest. It was also always the most useful.

What struck Ray most about these gatherings was not any single insight; it was the tone. People spoke honestly. They held each other to account without tearing each other down. They collaborated on problems they each could have struggled through alone. The room had a quality he had not seen in many professional settings:

genuine trust. Not the performative kind, not the kind built on contracts and liability, but the kind built on showing up week after week and telling the truth.

That, he realized, was what had been missing from his firm all along. Not better systems. Not better marketing. Trust and accountability, shared among people who actually cared about the outcome.

Tom Becomes a Teacher

Of all the changes Ray had made in the past year, none surprised him more than what happened with Tom.

Tom was twenty-eight, quick and capable, with a talent for systems and process that Ray had never properly recognized or cultivated. Under the old Ray, the one who delegated tasks without context and managed by output rather than by understanding, Tom had been a competent employee who was also quietly frustrated and quietly planning his exit.

Under the new Ray, he became something else entirely.

The change had started simply: Ray began explaining why. Why a particular client needed to be handled a certain way. Why the onboarding sequence mattered. Why certain reports were worth three hours, and others were not worth thirty minutes. Tom absorbed this context and began applying it on his own, making judgment calls that Ray had previously kept for himself, because he had never trusted anyone else to understand the reasoning behind them.

Within six months, Tom was solving problems before Ray even saw them. He had rebuilt the client onboarding process from scratch, cutting the average time to first deliverable by nearly two weeks. He had identified a workflow bottleneck that had been quietly adding four hours to every project the firm ran, invisible until someone finally looked for it.

One Thursday evening, Tom came to the group not as Ray's employee but as a contributor in his own right. He walked the table through the onboarding redesign, observation, Five Whys Root Cause Analysis, process change, measured result. The people around the table were nodding and taking notes.

Ray sat near the back and watched Tom teach the same lessons he had learned on a bench outside a coffee shop, in Tom's own words, from Tom's own experience.

After the meeting, Estella, who had come for the first time, curious about what had so completely taken over her husband's Thursday evenings, found Ray near the door watching the room empty out.

"You look like a man who found what he was looking for," she said.

"I think I did," he said. "Or part of it."

"What is the other part?"

He looked at her. "Making sure you know that none of this means anything to me without you in it."

She took his arm as they walked out into the cold Prescott evening, and said in her quiet and certain way: "I know, Ray. I have always known."

Part Six: What Success Looks Like

The Letter Ray Wrote to Himself

On the first anniversary of his conversation at the bench, Ray got up before the house woke, made coffee, and sat at the kitchen table with his journal.

He had decided to write himself a letter. He would read it every year on this date. A check-in. A measurement of distance traveled.

To Ray, one year from today and every year after:

Here is what I know now that I did not know a year ago:

Success is not a destination. I used to think of it as a place I would eventually arrive; a revenue number, a reputation of a certain size, a firm that ran itself while I took Fridays off. I now understand that this is completely wrong. Success is a direction, not a destination. It is the daily orientation of your life toward what matters, and the daily practice of asking whether you are still pointed that way.

What matters, for me, is this:

Faith and purpose, first. I believe that I am here for a reason, not a grand or famous reason, but a specific and ordinary one. I am here to do honest work, to lead the people in my care toward their own better versions, to keep my word and keep my books and keep my door open to people who need what I have. I do not know the full shape of why I was made the way I was made. But I believe there is a shape, and I believe the practice of improvement, the daily honest asking, is how I find it.

Family, second. Estella is not the background of my success. She is the ground of it. A life built without her full flourishing in it would be nothing I would want. When I ask whether I am succeeding, the first measure is whether she is well and truly known, not just loved, but known. There is a difference, and I let too many years pass before I understood it.

*Legacy, third. Not press mentions. Not awards.
Tom. The Thursday group. Moose's walls
opening up, slowly. Paul making considered
decisions. Mitch still sitting in the middle of every
room, watching everything, occasionally saying
the thing that changes how someone sees their
situation. Cole, still fighting for the people who
need someone in their corner. These are the
things that outlast me. They are the only things
that outlast me. I want to be careful with them.*

*Freedom and security, fourth. I want enough. I
know now what enough means for me; it is not a
number but a feeling: the absence of fear, the
presence of margin, the ability to be generous
without calculating the cost. I am closer to this
than I was. I am not finished.*

*And underneath all of it, woven through
everything like wire through a frame, the
practice. The daily, humble, stubborn practice of
asking: what can be better? Not what can be
more. What can be better?*

*Better work. Better leadership. A better husband.
A better father. A better friend, even to Moose,
who needs the kind of friendship that gently
refuses his fear. A better member of this
community that has given me so much.*

*I am not a wise man. I am a man who has
learned to ask better questions and is still
learning.*

That is enough. That is, in fact, everything.

— Ray

He folded the letter and tucked it into the back of the journal.

Estella came downstairs as the winter sun was coming up, found him at the table, and looked at his face with her quiet, accurate eyes.

"Good morning," she said.

"Yes," he said. "It is."

The Second Conversation

Spring came back to Prescott. The oak tree outside the coffee shop across from the courthouse square leafed out again, and Nona returned to her outdoor bench with her large coffee and her patient calm, as if winter had been merely an interruption.

Ray came on a Wednesday morning, early.

"One year," he said, sitting down.

"I know," she said. "I have been watching."

"What do you see?"

She looked at him for a long moment, the kind of look that does not flatter and does not diminish but simply sees.

"A man who stopped carrying the stone," she said.

"It is still there," he said. "But it feels different now. More like ballast. Something that keeps me from drifting away from what matters."

"Yes." She nodded. "That is what happens when you stop fighting the weight of your own questions and start using them."

He was quiet for a moment. "Can I ask you something I have wanted to ask for a year?"

"Of course."

"Why did you stop me that morning? You had seen me walk past a hundred times. Why that day?"

Nona looked at him for a long moment. A small smile crossed her face.

"Because you were walking slowly," she said. "You had already started asking the question yourself, in your body, even though your mind had not caught up yet. When a man walks slowly through a town he has walked through at a run for twenty years, he is almost ready to stop." She sipped her coffee. "I just gave him a place to sit."

Ray looked out across the street. The courthouse square and the morning traffic and the long familiar rhythms of a town where people were trying to build something worth having.

"Thank you," he said. "For the place to sit."

"Thank Estella," Nona said. "She told you to start walking."

Ray laughed; a real laugh, full and unguarded, the kind he did not laugh often enough.

"She did," he said.

Epilogue

They say that in Prescott, to this day, there is a gathering.

Once a week, on Thursday evenings, a group of business owners, consultants, attorneys, and professionals meet in a private dining room in a downtown restaurant. They bring their problems and their questions and their honest assessments of their own work. They speak without pretending. They listen without competing. They leave better than they arrived.

No one can quite remember when it started. The regulars speak vaguely of a performance consultant who ran a firm on Main Street and carried a restlessness in his chest, and one morning walked outside without his phone and stopped at a bench.

His wife still lives in the house on the east side of town. His former office manager runs the firm now, and runs it better than it has ever been run before. His five friends are all still with him, changed, each of them, in ways that are hard to measure and impossible to mistake.

Two of them are attorneys: one who fights for corporations and one who fights for families and small businesses. Both of them, on Thursday evenings, sit around the same table and ask the same honest questions. The law they practice is different. The practice of looking clearly at something and asking how it can be better, that part is the same.

The gathering has no official name.

The people of Prescott call it the Sharpening.

Because a life that is never examined grows dull. And a dull life, as any honest professional can tell you, is not the life you worked so hard to build.

Sharpen it. Sharpen it daily. Not in dramatic gestures, but in small honest acts; the question asked, the record kept, the mistake examined, the credit released, the person beside you truly seen.

That is the whole of it.

That is, it turns out, more than enough.

The End.

The Moral of the Fable

On improvement:

You cannot improve what you do not observe. Watch your own work with honest eyes. What you find will be uncomfortable and useful in equal measure.

On questions:

Ask what happened. Ask why it happened, and keep asking why until you reach the real root, not just the nearest symptom. Ask what if it were different. And ask, regularly and with courage: what am I refusing to see?

On the method behind the questions:

The Five Whys is not Ray's invention, or mine. It comes from the Toyota Production System and has been a tool of Lean practice for decades. Use it honestly. The honest part is the hard part.

On the people around you:

Your five, whoever yours are, will include people who excite you, people who polish the surface, people who have been there before, people who pull toward darkness, and people who see what you miss. All of them have something true to give you. None of them, alone, are enough.

On your anchor:

The person who keeps you grounded is not an obstacle to your growth. They are the ground itself. Do not forget to tend that ground.

On small changes:

Daily improvement, sustained, becomes transformation. Do not seek the single breakthrough. Seek the practice.

On trust and accountability:

You cannot build a culture of improvement alone. When the people around you feel safe enough to tell the truth about what is broken, what is working, and what they do not know, the whole team moves forward together. That is the collaborative spirit that turns individual effort into lasting change.

On success:

It is not a destination. It is a direction. Know what you are pointing toward: faith and purpose, family, legacy, security, meaningful work, and ask, daily, whether you are still pointed there.

On purpose:

You are here for something specific. Not something famous. Something faithful. The practice of improvement is how you find out what it is.

On the stone in your chest:

If you carry a restlessness, a feeling that good is not yet as good as it could be, do not silence it. It is not a sign that something is wrong. It is a sign that something more is possible. Use it.

About the Author

— ✦ —

Steve Aldridge: Facilitator & Coach

Steve Aldridge has spent his career doing what Ray spent a year learning to do, asking better questions, finding the root of the problem, and helping people and organizations become better versions of themselves.

He is the founder of Aldridge Performance Advisory LLC, where the belief is simple: real success comes from solving the right problems, empowering people, and building a culture of excellence. Steve partners with businesses to deliver practical solutions and lasting results, working at the intersection of strategy, process, and people. His practice is built on the conviction that sustainable improvement is less about tools and more about culture.

Drawing on a deep foundation in Lean Six Sigma (Black Belt certified) and decades of leadership across service organizations large and small, Steve specializes in cultural transformation and performance improvement through collaboration, strategic planning, and process design. A Summa

Cum Laude graduate of Northern Arizona University with a B.S. in Strategic Leadership, he brings both the credentials and the lived experience to deliver meaningful change in complex environments.

Faith-centered, mission-driven, and people-focused, Steve is a dedicated husband, father, and grandfather. He and his wife reside in Saint Charles, Missouri, where they strive to invest daily in both the professional and the personal, because, as Ray learned, the two are never really separate.

If any part of Ray's story felt familiar, the restlessness, the recurring problems, the quiet sense that something good could be something better, you are not alone. That is exactly the work we do. Reach out anytime. The conversation is always free.

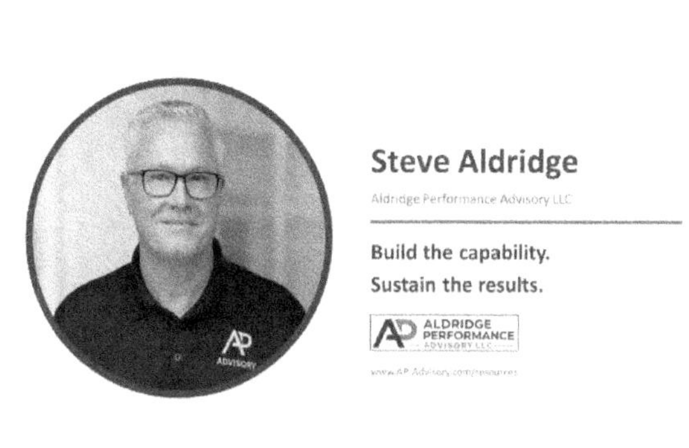

Aldridge Performance Advisory LLC

Steve@AP-Advisory.com | www.AP-Advisory.com